ISBN: 9781313200509

Published by:
HardPress Publishing
8345 NW 66TH ST #2561
MIAMI FL 33166-2626

Email: info@hardpress.net
Web: http://www.hardpress.net

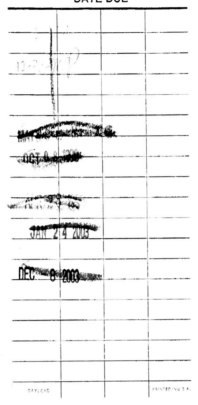

COMPOSITION

A SERIES OF EXERCISES SELECTED
FROM A NEW SYSTEM OF
ART EDUCATION
BY

ARTHUR W. DOW

Instructor in Art at Pratt Institute and at the
Art Students' League of New York

ΣΥΝΘΕΣΙΣ

PART I

FIFTH EDITION

NEW YORK

THE BAKER AND TAYLOR COMPANY

33 East Seventeenth Street

1903

CONTENTS

NOTE

THE title "Composition" has been given to this book because the system of art instruction which it represents has come to be commonly known by that name. The term "Composition" is, however, too limited, as the system in its full development includes, not only so-called composition, but all stages of the creation of a work of space-art. But as the following exercises relate to the fundamental process in such a creation, viz., the putting together of lines and masses, we will, for the present, accept the popular name.

This is the first publication of any consecutive series based upon the scheme of art education whose elements are here presented.

The history of the movement is as follows: Some nine years ago, after a course in the schools of Paris, I entered upon a comparative study of the art of all nations and epochs, in the hope of finding more light on composition in painting, and, incidentally, a better method of teaching than the prevailing nature-copying. While seeking for examples of Japanese art I met Professor Ernest F. Fenollosa, then curator of the unrivalled Oriental collection in the Boston Museum of Fine Arts.

He had had exceptional opportunities for a critical knowledge of both Eastern and Western art, and as a result of his research and comparisons, guided by a brilliant mind's clear grasp of fundamental ideas, had gained a new conception of art itself. He believed Music to be, in a sense, the key to the other fine arts, since its essence is pure beauty; that space-art may be called "visual music," and may be criticised and studied from this point of view. Following this new conception, he had constructed an art-educational system radically different from those whose corner-stone is Realism. Its leading thought is the expression of Beauty, not Representation.

I at once felt the truth and reasonableness of his position, and after much preparation in adapting these new methods to practical use, I began teaching a class in Boston, with Professor Fenollosa's co-operation. Here for the first time in this country, Japanese art materials were used for educational purposes.

After a few years of quiet effort and experiment in this way, Mr. Frederic B. Pratt of Brooklyn became interested in the results attained by this class, and as a consequence, the work was transferred in 1895 from my Boston studio to Pratt Institute, where in a progressive atmosphere, with large opportunity and hearty coöperation, it has reached a development already well known.

NOTE The art-instruction of modern days, an out-growth of the theories of Leonardo da Vinci, and the practice of later Renaissance and French academic artists, is too largely scientific. The pupil, from the very beginning, is forced to concentrate his energies upon acquiring a knowledge of various facts and processes. Self-expression is usually deferred till he has "learned to draw," till he has been through a course of cast-drawing, perspective, history, anatomy, history of costume, etc., — a thoroughly scientific drill related chiefly to Realism. After all this, he attempts to combine the knowledge and the skill in artistic expression, or in other words, a composition. Unless appreciation has developed despite the crowding of other things, the chances are that his work will lack the one vital element for which art exists, and to which he has as yet given slight attention — that is, Beauty.

But in this new view, art study is the gaining of an experience, and art instruction is the guiding of tendencies toward appreciation, and the training of mind and hand to create. This guidance and training, we believe, can be given by a series of exercises beginning, as in Music, with the simplest. In fact, the main idea in the system is to help the pupil at the very outset to originate a beautiful arrangement, say — a few lines harmoniously grouped together — and then proceed onward step by step to greater appreciation and fuller power of expression.

During this course, skill in drawing will come as a natural growth, and knowledge of perspective and all other requisites will be sought as the developing artistic faculty feels the need of them. In a word, instead of spending most of the effort on drawing, and then adding original work, or Composition, we begin with Composition, and find that it will lead to all the rest.

It is not my intention to furnish a book from which art may be taught, but to offer a principle by which an instructor can be guided, and exercises and examples suggestive of ways of carrying out the principle.

While the book will be of special service to those who have already had training in this method, to those who have not, it will I hope, afford many new ideas, and a mode of self-education.

The author is greatly indebted to his pupils, who have so kindly offered examples of their work, and also to friends who have in various ways assisted in the production of this book.

ARTHUR WESLEY DOW

New York, 1898

LINE-DRAWING AND MATERIALS

THE first step in the Art of Painting is the drawing of lines as the boundaries of shapes. These lines may be straight or curved, wide, thin, rough or sharp, faint or firm; they may be frankly left in the finished work, as in Japanese prints and early Italian frescoes, or they may appear merely as the edges of tones, as in a modern landscape painting or a charcoal sketch. But in the making of these lines there is opportunity for great beauty of proportion, and a powerful, vital touch, full of personality. Examples are here given of lines by various great masters.

The line of Soga Shubun, Nos. 1 and 2, is bold and strong, and varies with each object drawn. The character and texture of houses, rocks, trees and marsh grass are suggested in the line.

The line of Sesshu, Nos. 3 and 4, is angular, rugged, and vibrating with the nervous force of the artist's hand.

The line of Kano Yusho, No. 5, is graceful, but sharp and crisp.

The school of Kano Tanyu, Nos. 6, 7, 8, and 9, is readily recognized by the peculiar quality of the slap-dash, picturesque line. Okumura Masanobu, No. 10, puts into his simple curves the classic purity of Greek line.

Michelangelo's great Titanic lines, No. 11, are well calculated to express the su-

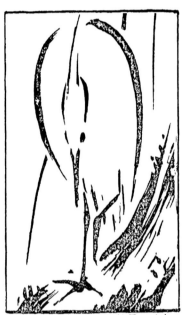

Nº 6 Part of a sketch from book of the Tanyu school

perhuman beings of his compositions. Leonardo's, No. 12, combine delicacy and absolute power.

Millet's strength lies largely in his line. There is more than truth in it; there is beauty and character and intense meaning. (No. 13.)

To produce lines so expressive requires complete control of the hand, guided by a disciplined creative mind. It therefore seems proper that the student should, at the outset, enter upon a training that will give him such control and discipline.

7

LINE-
DRAWING
AND
MATERIALS

There are many implements for drawing lines, but the one which responds most readily, gives the widest range of quality and tends soonest to make the hand obey the will, is the Japanese brush. The sizes generally used are shown in the illustration:

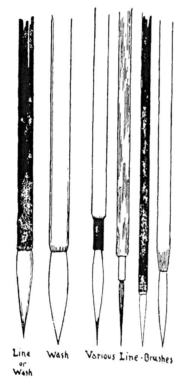

Line
or
Wash   Wash   Various Line-Brushes

The long brushes are best for long lines, the short ones for sharp corners and broken lines. The "painting brush" is here meant, not the Chinese "writing brush" which is worthless for this purpose.

Japanese paper is to be preferred, as it is specially prepared with glue-size, and so takes the ink better than any other, is beautiful in color and texture and thin enough for tracing. I have found unprinted wall paper very serviceable for practice:—it has a good surface and is cheap. The best ink is the Japanese, ground on the ink-stone, but other inks or even black water-color may be used. Place a few drops of water on the ink-stone, and rub the stick of ink on the slant till intense blackness results. Dry the stick at once and wrap it in paper. Never leave it soaking, or it will crumble to pieces.

DRAWING THE LINE

Pin your paper very smoothly upon a board, or dampen and paste it by the edges. If the brush is new, it must be washed and dried, as the maker puts starch into it to keep the point. Dipping a wet brush into the ink, of course grays and weakens the tone.

The board may be laid upon the knee or on a desk: it can be flat or slightly inclined. Keep the head up and away from it. Take the brush between thumb and middle finger, as shown in the illustration, steadying it with the fore-finger.

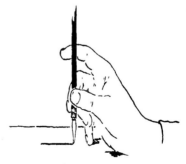

Manner of holding the Brush

8

No. 1. — Soga Shubun, Japanese, XV century (part of screen)

LINES BY
VARIOUS
MASTERS
(See page 7)
The Japanese ex-
amples on pages 9, 10,
11 (except No. 4), and
on pages 33, 40, are
from the collections
in the Museum of
Fine Arts, Boston.

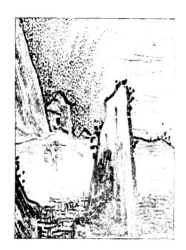

No. 2 — Soga Shubun

No. 3. — Sesshu, Japanese, XV century

No. 4. — Sesshu (Japanese) XV century

No. 5. — Kano Yusho, XVII century (fragment)

No. 9. — Kano Tanyu, XVII century (fragment)

No. 8. — Kano Naonobu, XVII century (fragment)

Michelangelo

No. 7. — Kano Yasunobu, XVII century (fragment)

Michelangelo

LINES BY
VARIOUS
MASTERS
(See page 7)

No. 12 — Leonardo da Vinci (Louvre)

No. 11. — Michelangelo

No. 13. — J. F. Millet

Dip it into the ink, and holding it perpendicular to the paper, draw your line. It must be held in a perpendicular position in order to move freely in all directions as does the etcher's needle.

The line is not drawn with the fingers, but by a movement of the whole hand and arm

in one sweep. This gives greater force. The hand may be steadied if necessary by resting the end of the little finger on the paper.

Determine the width of the line at the start, by pressing the brush-point firmly down till it spreads to the desired width. Slowness of drawing is most important, as an expressive or artistic line is not made by mere momentum of the hand, but by pure force of will controlling the hand. In slow drawing, the line can be watched and guided as it grows under the brush-point.

Slight waverings, when not resulting from weakness or nervousness, are not objectionable; in fact, may add to the individuality and expressiveness of the line.

Nº 10 Okumura Masanobu (Japanese) 18ª cent.

Good lines - drawn very slowly with unaided hand

Poor, weak lines - quickly drawn

Brush in wrong position

Ruled lines hence of no artistic value

Examples of both good and faulty lines are shown on preceding page.

EXERCISE

As the straight line is the simplest, the pupils should begin with that and practice until they can draw it freely, remembering that straightness of direction is the essential point, not mere geometric straightness. In beginning, the lines can be about one-eighth or one-fourth inch wide and must be kept of uniform width throughout. Let them draw not only isolated lines but sets of parallels, also squares, etc., as in the illustration.

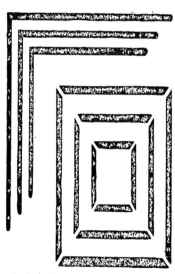

Practice-lines drawn with Japanese Brush (reduced ½)

Copying some of the lines by the masters would be valuable, if done, not for the sake of a facsimile, but in the endeavor to reach the same power and feeling.

The aim of this exercise is to put the hand under control of the will, but it should not be carried too far, as all the succeeding problems will tend to the same end.

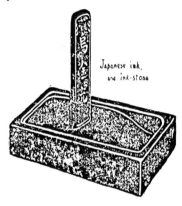

Japanese ink, and ink-stone

A STARTING POINT

A work of fine art, in one view at least, is a result of Appreciation combined with Power to express.

Neither of these can be gained by methods of scientific study; on the contrary, they are the birthright of every human being and can be developed by training.

The most natural course of training is that which begins with the simple elements of an art and leads on gradually to its more complex problems. The student who is set down before an outdoor landscape and directed to paint it, is at once embarrassed by many different kinds of obstacles; the choice of the subject, placing it on the canvas, managing the darks, mixing the colors, handling the brush, all confuse him because he is attempting an advanced stage of his art, and lacks education and experience.

LINE
DRAWING
AND
MATERIALS
—A START-
ING POINT

The thought of the present system is that the many different acts and processes that go to make up a painting may be attacked and mastered singly, and thereby a power gained to handle them unconsciously when they present themselves all together in an advanced work.

In the Art of Painting there are three elements by which beauty may be created:

1. LINE—that is, the boundaries of the shapes.
2. DARK AND LIGHT MASSES.
3. COLOR.

(The first two only will be considered in this book.)

The beginner might take up any one of these and compose in it, or he might take all three together in their simplest form. But as Dark-and-Light and Color are directly dependent upon Line, it seems most reasonable to begin with Line, and to become somewhat familiar with the putting together of lines and the harmonizing of sizes and areas, before attempting the other two.

Among the many kinds of lines used to bound areas, the straight line is the simplest, and here we have found a starting point for a series of progressive studies. If the pupil can create even a little beauty with a few straight lines, he is on the way to great possibilities, for it must be remembered that in this seemingly limited field are to be found works of the highest order, from the Greek fret to Giotto's Tower.

This is not the only starting point. There are many others, but we will choose this and begin our series with Straight Line Composition.

A Study in Proportion — effect of different spacing and grouping

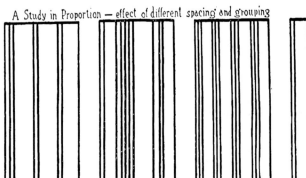

LINE COMPOSITION

I.—SQUARES

PAINTING is a space art. It is concerned with the breaking up of a space into parts which vary in shape, depth of tone and color.

In choosing a space for first attempts at Composition, we shall take one of the simplest — the square. It is bounded by straight lines and its proportions cannot be varied. We will use vertical and horizontal lines of uniform width. The beauty that will result from such elements must be a beauty of proportion, a harmony of well-cut space, a little musical theme in straight lines and grouped areas.

If a square is cut at regular intervals — No. 14 — no art can be manifested as long as it is in outline only. But with irregular intervals there is room for inventive genius, and the square may be cut symmetrically — No. 15 — or unsymmetrically No. 16. In the first case we have the kind of beauty seen in panellings, etc.; in the second, plaids and ginghams.

EXERCISE

Let the pupil draw a square in pencil or charcoal, purely by the eye, no measurement of any kind being used. Then cut it by vertical and horizontal lines. He can choose one way of arranging his lines, his theme, so to speak — say No. 17 — and then see how many variations he can make, keeping the same general plan. This exercise may be much prolonged, if necessary, but the pupil must constantly set up a row of his drawings and compare them, picking out the best. For instance, make six arrangements on the plan of No. 17. Then choose the best.

The instructor will help in this critical judgment. The selected drawings may be still further improved; then stretch Japanese paper smoothly over them and trace in firm, black ink-lines, with the unaided hand. Continue the tracing until the drawings are as good as possible in proportion and the line executed with feeling for artistic quality.

Avoid hard mechanical lines and all that savors of rule and compass or laborious painstaking. Never try to erase an ink line; — if a mistake occurs begin a new tracing.

The examples show a few of the various ways in which this problem has been worked out by students and others.

This exercise if carried on under competent criticism, will have begun in a small way a development of

1. The Inventive Faculties.
2. Appreciation of Beauty, and
3. Power of Expression,

being purely and wholly an artistic effort.

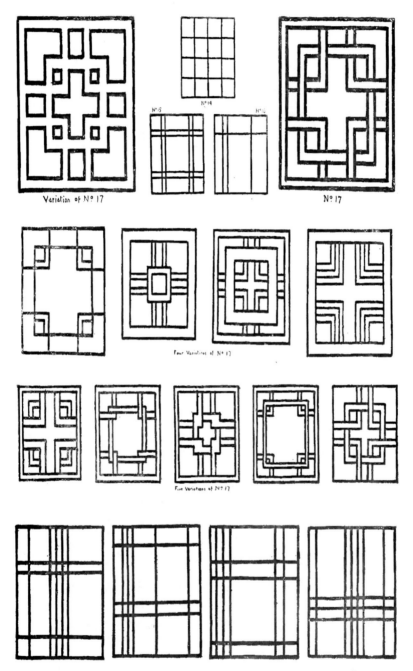

Variation of Nº 17

Nº 14

Nº 15   Nº 16

Nº 17

Four Variations of Nº 17

Five Variations of Nº 17

LINE COMPOSITION

II.—VARIATION

THE subject of Variation receives little or no attention in the ordinary academic course of art education, but it is a fundamental idea in this system.

The great masters of music have shown the infinite possibilities of combination and varied expression:—the same theme appears again and again with new beauty, with different quality and with complex accompaniments. Even so can lines, masses and colors be wrought into musical forms and endlessly varied. The Japanese color-print exemplifies this, each copy of the same subject being varied in shade or hue or disposition of masses to suit the restless inventive energy of its author. In old Italian textiles the same pattern appears repeatedly, but varied in size, proportion, dark-and-light and color. The artistic mind is always trying new ways of expressing a beautiful idea. In times when art is decadent, the designers and painters lack inventive power and merely imitate nature or the creations of others. Then comes Realism, conventionality, and the death of art.

The art education which this book advocates would reveal to the student the boundless possibilities of his mind, and teach him to avoid the conventional and the commonplace. It would show him that poverty of ideas is no characteristic of the artist and that no work is of value unless it expresses the personality of its creator. That which anybody can do is not worth doing. If your drawing is just like your neighbor's it has no value as art. The work of all masters of fine art is intensely individual, full charged with mighty personality. A study of variation tends to the very opposite of the conventional and the commonplace—to a finding for one's self ever new ways of expression.

EXERCISE

In the last chapter Variation was introduced, but only in the interior lines, as a square is not variable. A step beyond this is to choose a shape where both the boundary and the interior lines are variable. The Rectangle is one such shape, —it is self-evident that the modifications of its proportions can be numberless. The composition of lines in this shape can be treated in two ways:

1. The Rectangles being made all of the same size and proportion, but interior lines varied, as in No. 18.

2. The same Interior system but the border varied, as in No. 19.

The instructor chooses some simple arrangement of vertical and horizontal lines within a rectangle, sketches the idea upon the blackboard for the class to draw in pencil or charcoal, and requires them to

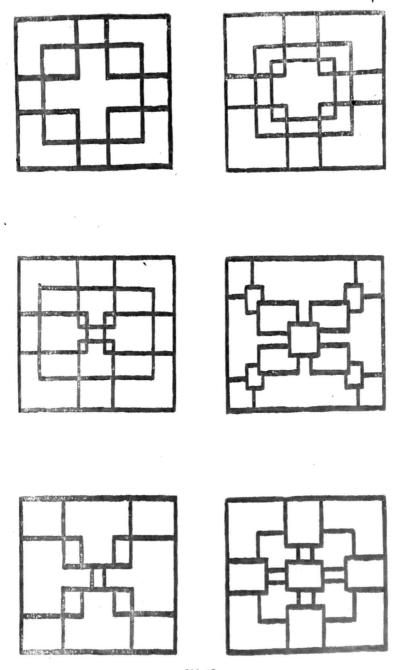

N° 18

make a number of variations upon it as indicated above and in the examples.

The best designs are to be traced in ink in lines of equal width throughout.

From previous experience the pupils will show better judgment in arranging the lines and areas, and more appreciation of good proportion. The difference between a commonplace design and a beautiful one may be very slight — it can be felt, but not described.

Study the illustrations given herewith; use any or all of them as themes for Variation. This exercise admits of very great expansion according to the age of pupils and the limits of time.

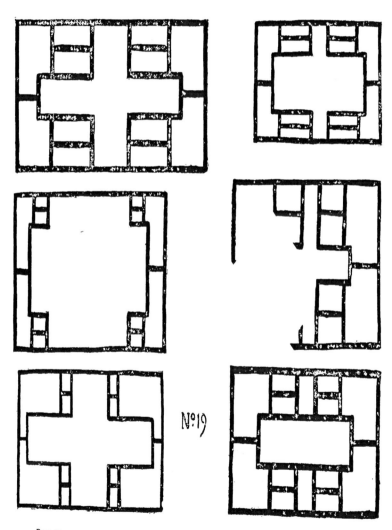

Nº19

LINE COMPOSITION

III.—EXAMPLES OF BEAUTIFUL STRAIGHT LINE ARRANGEMENT

AN important part of an art education is the coming in contact with the best works of art, and getting from them an appreciation of beauty and a stimulus to create. The pupil too often listens to talk about the subject of the picture, or the history, derivation and meaning of the design, or the accuracy and likeness to nature of the drawing. All these are really either literary or scientific considerations, and, while they have their place, touch upon art only superficially. The most important fact relating to a great work of fine art is that it is beautiful; and the best way to help the pupil to see and appreciate that beauty is to call his attention to it as an illustration of a principle. Let him see what a master has done with the very problem which he is trying to work out. If you have given him curved line composition as a subject, show him one of the best examples of it that the world has ever known,—the Victory of Samothrace. His previous efforts to evolve compo-sitions of curves will at once give him the key to an appreciation of the statue. The purpose of the present exercise is to show the student how the simple straight-line beauty of which we have been speaking may appear in things great and small, from a cathedral tower to a cupboard shelf. The campanile of the Cathedral of Flor-

ence, No. 20, designed by that master of architecture and painting, Giotto, is a rectangular composition of exceeding beauty. Its charm lies chiefly in its delicately harmonized proportions on a straight-line scheme. It is a music of lines and spaces. The areas are largest at the top, diminishing downwards by subtle changes and variations. The graceful mouldings, the window tracery, the many tones of marble and porphyry, are but the finish, an embroidery, so to speak, on the splendid main lines of the structure.

A Venetian palace of early period, No. 21, presents this rectangular beauty in an entirely different way. First, a vertical line divides the façade into two unequal but balanced proportions; each of these is again divided by horizontal lines and by windows and balconies into smaller spaces, the whole forming a perfect harmony—each part related to, and affected by, every other part.

The wall of honor of a Japanese room is arranged in this same rectangular fashion, No. 22. A vertical line, as in the Venetian palace façade, divides the whole space into two—one of these is further divided into shelved recesses, or cabinets with sliding doors; the other is for pictures (kakemono), no more than three of which are hung at a time.

LINE COM-
POSITION
III.—EX-
AMPLES OF
BEAUTIFUL
STRAIGHT
LINE AR-
RANGE-
MENT

No. 23 shows three of these shelf arrange-ments. As in their other design, the Jap-anese manifest no end of invention in the manner of filling this space. They pub-lish books with hundreds of designs, no two alike.

EXERCISE

If possible the student should in this case work from large photographs, but as they are not always accessible, we give here tracings from photographs of the build-ings mentioned, and from the original Japanese design-books.

Let the pupil copy these examples. In no better way can he be made to feel their refinement, and to perceive the art in them. An attempt to copy brings his mind for a little time into contact with that of a superior. He sees the difficulty of reaching the perfection of the master. Copying as a means of improving one's style, and a strengthening of the creative faculty, is the opposite of copying as a substitute for original work.

After making the most exact copies pos-sible (without any measurement what-ever), the pupil must invent designs of his own, on the same general plan, but varied as to the sizes of spaces, etc.

Let him try the Tower and the Palace with widely differing proportions. Let him see how many shelf arrangements he can originate.

This, and all these exercises, may be summed up in two words:

APPRECIATE

ORIGINATE

N.º 20
Giotto's Tower,
(traced from a
photograph)

Venetian Palace facade – main lines–(traced) N°21

Rectangular composition, Sideboard of XV cent. (traced from photo)

Part of the Tower of Seville
(Traced from a photograph)

N°22   Side of a Japanese room – (traced from an ancient book)

N°23

LINE COMPOSITION

IV.—LANDSCAPE

THE modern arbitrary division of Painting into Representative and Decorative has tended to put into the background that which we here call Composition, and to bring forward nature-imitating as a substitute. The picture-painter is led to think of likeness to nature as the most desirable quality for his work, and the designer talks of "conventionalising"; both judging their art by a standard of Realism rather than of Beauty. In the world's art epochs there was no such division. Every work of space-art was regarded as primarily an arrangement, with Beauty as its raison d'être. Even a portrait was first of all a composition, with the facts and the truth subordinate to the greater idea of a beauty of æsthetic structure. Training in the fundamental principles of Composition gave the artists a wide field — they were at once picture-painters, decorators, architects and sculptors. Giotto could embody his line-thoughts in glowing color on the walls of churches, or in the ivory-tinted marble of the peerless Campanile of Florence. Following this thought of the oneness of art, we find that the picture, the plan, and the pattern are alike in the sense that each is a group of synthetically related spaces. Abstract design is, as it were, the primer of painting, in which principles of Composition appear in a clear and definite form.

In the picture they are not so obvious, being found in complex interrelations and concealed under detail.

The designer and picture-painter start in the same way. Each has before him a blank space on which he sketches out the main lines of his composition. This may be called his Line-idea, and on it hinges the excellence of the whole, for no delicacy of tone, or harmony of color can remedy a bad proportion. A picture, then, may be said to be in its beginning actually a pattern of lines. Could the art student have this fact in view at the outset, it would save him much time and ill-directed energy. Nature will not teach him composition. The sphinx is not more silent than she on this point. He must learn the secret as Giotto and Francesca, and Kanawoka and Turner learned it, by the study of art itself in the works of the masters, and by continual creative effort. If students could have a thorough training in the elements of their profession they would not fall into the error of supposing that such a great universal idea as Beauty of Line could be compressed into a few cases like the "triangle," "bird's-wing," "line of beauty," or "scroll ornament," nor would they take these notions as a kind of receipt for composing the lines of pictures.

Insistence upon the placing of Arrange-

24

ment or Composition above Representation must not be considered as any undervaluation of the latter. The student may learn nature's forms, colors and effects, and how to represent them; he needs to know the properties of pigments, how to handle brushes and materials, perhaps the laws of perspective and anatomy. More or less of this knowledge and skill will be required in his career, but they are only helps to art, not substitutes for it, and we believe, as stated in the introduction to this book, that if he begins with Composition, that is, with a study of art itself, he will acquire these naturally, as he feels the need of them.

Returning now to our premise that the picture and the abstract design may show the same structural beauty, let us see how the simple idea of combining straight lines, as so far considered, may be illustrated by

No. 24

Landscape. Looking out from a grove we have trees as vertical straight lines, cutting lines horizontal or nearly so. Leaving small forms out of account we have in these main lines an arrangement of rectangular spaces much like the gingham

and other simple patterns. This then is one kind of beauty of landscape. To become more familiar with it, see the following:

EXERCISE

No. 24 is a landscape reduced to its simplest lines, all detail being omitted.

First make an enlarged copy of this. (In this way one works for proportion only, and cannot slavishly imitate. The same end is gained by making a reduced copy of a large drawing.) Then—to experience the creation of fine rectangular proportions in landscape, and the setting of the subject into a space—arrange this in rectangles of varying shape, some nearly square, others tall, others long and narrow horizontally, as in No. 25. To bring the whole landscape into all these will not, of course, be possible, but in each the essential lines must be retained in order not to change the subject.

Pupils should draw this exercise in ink after preliminary studies with pencil or charcoal, refining the proportions and correcting errors by tracing.

Then they may find in nature a similar subject, sketch it, and vary it in the same way.

It should be clearly understood that we are here using landscape merely as an illustration. The art of landscape painting is a special subject, not to be treated here, but we believe that the true way to approach it is through these or similar exercises.

First study the art, then apply it, whether to landscape or any other kind of expression.

N°25
(see p. 25)

LINE COMPOSITION

V.—EXAMPLES OF PICTURES COMPOSED ON RECTANGULAR LINES

GREAT architects and designers were not the only ones to use this simple line-idea—the masters of pictorial art have based upon it some of their best work.

No. 26 is a sketch from Whistler's "Battersea Bridge." It has but two principal lines, cutting the space into rectangles of beautiful proportion.

Puvis de Chavannes, in his mural paintings, expresses solemnity, majesty and repose by the vertical lines of his Elysian groves, cutting the level silhouettes or long horizontally sweeping curves. No. 27.

Hiroshige, the best of the later Japanese landscape composers, a man of inexhaustible inventive power, often uses the rectangular idea. Nos. 28 and 29. None of these examples need further explanation. They are beautiful, even when divested of color and dark-and-light, because they are built upon a few straight lines, finely related, and a few delicately proportioned areas.

EXERCISE

These examples can be treated in the following manner:—

1. Copy exactly—as nearly as can be done by the eye, without measurement.

2. Draw enlarged, keeping the same relative proportions.

3. Vary each of them by changing the proportion of the boundary and interior lines.

4. Find in nature a similar subject, and make many original compositions.

Draw all the best in ink, as usual.

Sketch of part of middle distance "L'Hiver" by Puvis de Chavannes

Sketch of part of painting by P. de Chavannes

Hiroshige (traced from a colored print) Nº 24

The Annunciation, Piero della Francesca. (tracing)

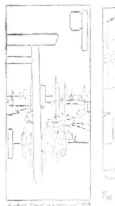

Hiroshige (traced from a colored print) Nº 19

Four examples of rectangular composition (See V pagr 27)

Drawn from fresco by Giotto (tracing)

Sketch from a picture by Whistler Nº 26

LINE COMPOSITION

VI.—REPETITION—OBLIQUE LINES

WE have thus far kept to one way of putting straight lines together, and we have found even that one to offer almost unlimited possibilities. There are at least seven other principles of straight-line composition, each of which would open a new series as vast as the one we have already considered.

For instance, Repetition, the rhythmical arrangement of lines at regular intervals, as in borders and surface patterns; or at irregular intervals, as in the kind of landscape shown in Nos. 31, 32 and 33. Repetition is a line-music of a very different character from that we have so far studied. It is, perhaps, the oldest form of design; the savage uses it when he ornaments his pottery with rows of straight marks.

Fragments of Indian pottery found at Ipswich Mass.

The development of this kind of composition is taken up in connection with Dark-and-Light, in Section XIV. Consult also the illustrations of Sections X and XI.

It is not necessary for the present to discuss more than one other way of composing straight-lines. Leaving the rectangular scheme, we will consider two uses of the Oblique line. Sometimes it softens a right angle, thus evolving the whole race of brackets and corner ornaments, in architecture, patterns, and decorations. Nos. 34, 35, etc.

Sometimes it is brought in in triangles, or combined with the rectangle, as in the pavements of Italian churches, and Arabic and other designs, Nos. 36, 37 and 38. See illustrations of Section X.

EXERCISE

The oblique line only will be studied here. First copy the examples of brackets, and all the designs where an oblique line is drawn or suggested for the sake of softening a right angle. Then find other examples in photograph, cast, books, buildings, or textiles, and make drawings of them, expressing the principle without useless detail. That is, reduce the examples to as few lines as possible.

Then make a series of original designs.

A second part of this exercise may be the composing of oblique line patterns in the spirit of the pavements of Italian churches

29

LINE COM·
POSITION
VI. — REPE·
TITION —
OBLIQUE
LINES

—the line-music of the little pieces of marble arranged in a mosaic of fine proportions. A good photograph of the pavement of St. Mark's, Venice, or that of the Cathedral of Murano, with a description of their richness of tone and color, would demonstrate to the student how great an art may lie in these apparently simple beginnings. Those designers had, perhaps, only the chips of white marble, of red and green porphyry, left by the builders of the church, but being familiar with the elements of art, with beauty of Line, Dark-and-Light and Color, they arranged their chips into beautiful patterns that may well be ranked as art of a high order.

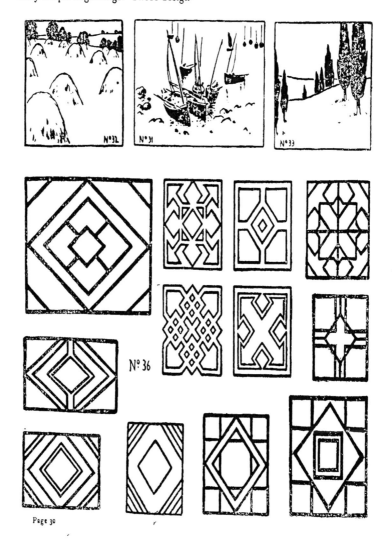

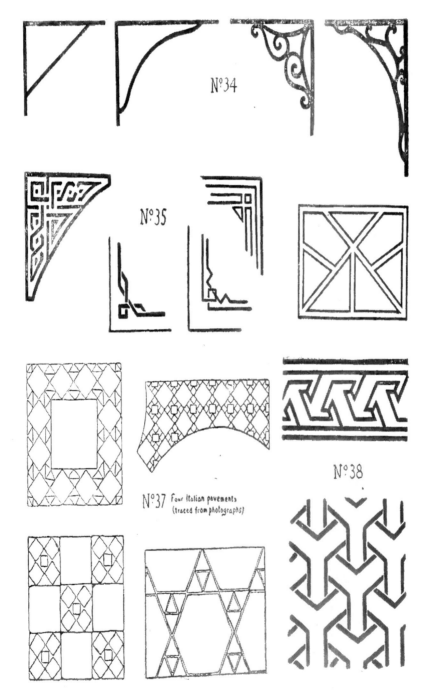

Nº34

Nº35

Nº37 Four Italian pavements
(traced from photographs)

Nº38

LINE COMPOSITION

VII.— LANDSCAPE ARRANGEMENT

IN Section IV the landscape was constructed on a rectangular line-scheme for the special purpose of emphasizing the intimate relation between elementary abstract design and pictorial design. The examples given in Section V showed the student the dignity and importance of these simple ideas of composition by letting him see how great artists have used them. Incidentally these lessons gave a clue to the appreciation of one class of pictorial art (including some Japanese prints), which might otherwise remain unrevealed for a long time.

The student must, however, be warned against mistaking a mere geometric combination of lines for an æsthetic combination. There is no special virtue in a rectangular scheme or any other in itself; it is the treatment of it that makes it art or not art. Many a commonplace architect has designed a tower similar to Giotto's, and many a dauber of oil paint has constructed a wood interior on a line-plan resembling that of Puvis. So the mere doing of the work recommended here will be of little value if the only thought is to get over the ground, or if the mind is intent upon names rather than principles. The doing of it well, with an artistic purpose in mind, is the true way and the only way to develop the creative faculties. Another reason for introducing landscape here is to offset the doctrine of the nature-imitators that accurate representation is a virtue of highest order and to be attained in the beginning. It is undeniably serviceable, but to start with it is to begin at the wrong end. It is not the province of the landscape painter merely to represent trees, hills and houses — so much topography — but to express an emotion, and this he must do by art. His art will be manifest in his composition, in his placing of his trees, hills and houses in synthetic relations to each other and to the space-boundary. Here is the strength of George Inness; to this he gave his chief effort. He omits detail, and rarely does more than to indicate the forms of things by a few touches.

This relation among the parts of a composition is what we call Beauty, and it begins to exist with the first few lines drawn. Even the student may express a little of it if he feels it, and the attempt to embody it in lines on paper will surely lead to a desire to know more fully the character and shapes of things. A young pupil who had been working in this way, said, "I don't know how to draw trees, but I mean to learn at once." She had the ideas; the effort to put them forth led her to seek a knowledge of drawing with enthusiasm and pleasure.

This case is but one of multitudes in my

32

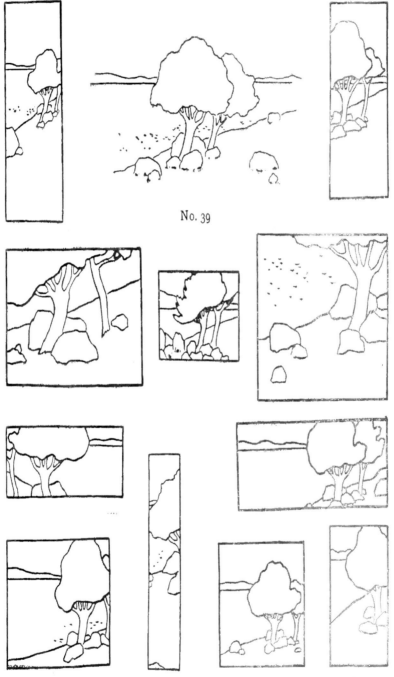

No. 39

LINE COM-
POSITION
VII. — LAND-
SCAPE
ARRANGE-
MENT

experience, witnessing to the soundness of the philosophy which underlies this system and offsetting that shallow saying of the realists, "It is time enough to think of composition after you can draw."

<u>EXERCISE</u>

The problem in this section is to be, in accordance with our progressive series, a step in advance of the one in Section IV. Leaving the rectangular idea, take any landscape that has some good elements in it, reduce it to a few main lines and strive to present it in the most beautiful way — for example the one in No. 39, or one drawn by the instructor, or even a tracing from a photograph. Remember that the aim is not to represent a place, nor to get good drawing now; put those thoughts out of the mind and try only to cut a space finely by landscape shapes; the various lines in your subject combine to enclose spaces, and the art in your composition will lie in placing these spaces in beautiful relations to each other. Here must come in the personal influence of the instructor, which is, after all, the very core of all art teaching. He can bring the pupils up to the height of his own appreciation, and perhaps no farther. The best of systems is valueless without this personal artistic guidance. At this stage of landscape composition, the idea of Grouping can be brought in, as a help in arranging sizes and shapes.

There is a certain beauty existing in a contrast of large and small. It is the opposite of Monotony. For instance, compare a street where there is variety in the sizes of buildings and trees, with another of rows of dull ugly tenement blocks. Ranges of hills, spires and pinnacles, clumps of large and small trees, clusters of haystacks, or even the disposition of things on a mantel, will serve to illustrate this idea.

Beware of making a universal rule out of this sort of composition (i.e. principal and subordinate), for there is another kind of beauty exactly opposite, in which the parts are all alike, or nearly so; for example, rows of willows, or Nos. 31, 32 and 33, in Section VI.

To discover the best arrangement, and to get the utmost experience in line and space composition, the landscape should be set into many boundaries of differing proportions, as in Section IV, and as shown in the examples, keeping the essential lines of the subject, but varying them to fit the boundary. For instance, a tree may be made taller in a high vertical space than in a low horizontal space.

After working out this exercise the pupil may draw a landscape from nature and treat it in the same way. Let him rigorously exclude detail, drawing only the outlines of objects.

DARK-AND-LIGHT COMPOSITION

VIII. — NOTAN

WE have considered the subject of Line in a very general way, and must leave it at this point, postponing for the present a detailed study of the separate principles, also the whole subject of Curved Line, and the composition of other varieties of Line except as they appear in the landscapes, flowers and patterns of these exercises.

It has already been stated that beauty in painting is manifested in three ways, namely by

LINE

DARK-AND-LIGHT

COLOR

We have now to consider the second of these elements, Dark-and-Light. There is no one word in English comprehensive enough to express what is here meant by this hyphened phrase, but as the Japanese have brought so much of this kind of beauty to our art we may well use their word for it, Notan. Besides, the adoption of a single word, and a new one, serves to emphasize our characterization of it as a great æsthetic element. Thus the Notan of a pattern or a picture is the arrangement of the dark and light masses. Artists often employ the word "spotting" in this sense, and sometimes the more indefinite word "effect," while "wash-out" designates in studio slang the lack of this element.

The Orientals, who have never considered the representation of shadows as of serious importance, have recognized Notan as a special and vital part of the art of painting, to be studied for its own sake, a field for creative activity entirely distinct from Line or Color. Some of their schools discarded color, and for ages painted in ink, so mastering Notan as to attract the admiration, and profoundly influence the art of the western world.

Yet so firmly is our art embedded in the traditions of the nature-imitators, that Dark-and-Light is not considered in school curricula, except in its limited application to the representation of things. The study of "light and shade" has for its aim, not the creation of a beautiful idea in terms of contrasting masses of light and dark, but merely the accurate rendering of certain facts of nature, — hence is a scientific rather than an artistic exercise. The pupil who begins in this way will be embarrassed in advanced work by lack of experience in arranging and differentiating tones. Worse than that, it tends to cut him off from the appreciation of one whole class of great works of art. As in the case of Line, so again in this is manifest the narrowness and weakness of the scheme of nature-imitating as a foundation for art education. The Realistic standard has tended, and ever will tend, to the decay of art.

To attain an appreciation of Notan, and power to create with it, the following fundamental fact must be understood, namely, that a placing together of masses of dark and light, synthetically related, conveys to the eye an impression of beauty entirely independent of meaning. For example, squares of dark porphyry against squares of light marble, checks in printed cloth, and blotty ink sketches by the Venetians, the Dutch, and the Japanese.

When this occurs accidentally in nature, as in the case of a grove of dark trees against a light hillside, or a pile of dark buildings against a twilight sky, we at once perceive its beauty, and say that the scene is "picturesque." This quality, which makes the natural scene a good subject for a picture, is analogous to music. Truthful drawing and "conscientiousness" would have nothing to do with an artist's rendering of this. This is the kind of "visual music" which the Japanese so love in the rough ink painting of their old masters, where there is but a mere hint of facts.

Claude Lorraine and Corot, in the West, Kakei and Sesshu in the East, owe the light of their skies and the mystery of their groves to an appreciation of the refinements of Notan. The etchers, the illustrators, and the practical designers are equally dependent upon it.

The modern art student, feeling the necessity of a knowledge of Dark-and-Light when he begins to make original compositions, has open to him but one resource, that of sketching the "spotting" as he calls it, of good designs and pictures, — see page 53 and Section XIX, — an excellent practice, if followed understandingly. I believe that the difficulty may be overcome:

1. By acknowledging Notan as an element distinct from Line or Color.

2. By attempting its mastery by progressive stages which shall lead to appreciation.

As in the case of Line, isolate its simplest manifestations, create with them, and then proceed onward to the higher problems.

DARK-AND-LIGHT COMPOSITION

IX.—NOTAN OF LINE

AS long as the lines of a design are kept of uniform width, the beauty is limited to proportion of areas and quality of touch, but widen some of the lines, and at once appears a new grace, Dark-and-Light. The textile designers who are restricted to straight lines, have recourse to this principle. They widen lines, vary their depth of tone, glorify them with color, and show that what seems a narrow field is really one of wide range.

EXERCISE

Choose some of the previous geometric line patterns, and widen certain of the lines, as illustrated in the plate. Incidentally this will give good brush practice, as the lines are to be drawn at one stroke. Push the point of the brush down to the required width, then draw the line. Try a large number of arrangements, set them up in a row and pick out the best.

In choosing and criticising, remember that every part of a work of art has something to say. If one part is made so prominent that the others have no reason for being there, the art is gone. So in this case; if one line asserts itself to the detriment of the others, there is discord. There may be many or few lines, but each must have its part in the whole.

In a word, wholeness is essential to beauty; it distinguishes Music from Noise.

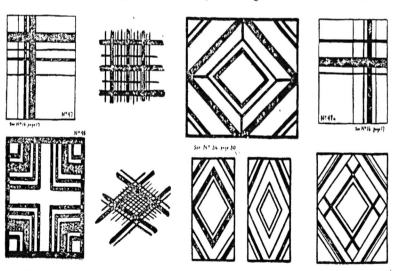

Page 38

No. 40. — Sesshu (see Sections VIII and XXIV, also pages 9 and 10)

No. 42. — Kakei

No. 41. — Yoiu (Sesshu school)

N.º 43

Seymour Haden

J. M^cN. Whistler

N.º 44 - Ippo, - Japanese, Shijo school.

N.º 45a - Constable

Harpignies

N.º 45

Daubigny

Compositions by various masters, showing Notan arrangement (Sections VIII, XIX, also page 53)

DARK-AND-LIGHT COMPOSITION

X. — NOTAN OF TWO TONES — STRAIGHT-LINE PATTERNS

THE last chapter treated of the transition from Line to Dark-and-Light by means of Notan of Line. In this we enter in good earnest upon a study of this important element, working from simple to complicated.

As in the case of Line, there may be many starting points. One might begin by blotting ink or charcoal upon paper, by copying the darks and lights from photographs of masterpieces, etc., but we will select the straight-line pattern and the flat black ink wash as more in harmony with our series, and a starting point that experience has proved to be satisfactory.

The aim must be to feel and understand Notan as something by which beauty may be created, hence it is best to avoid Representation at first — not to confound Notan with "light and shade," "modelling," or anything that refers to the imitation of natural objects.

Having found a straight-line pattern which is fine in its proportions, we will add to it this new kind of beauty, and as much of it as can be expressed by the extremes of Notan, black against white. It is apparent that we cannot reduce Dark-and-Light to simpler terms than these two tones.

The beginner may imagine that not much can be done with flat black against flat white, but let him examine the decorative design of the world. He will find the black and white check and patterns derived from it, in old velvets of Japan, in the woven and printed textiles of all nations, in marble floors, inlaid boxes and architectural ornament. Departing from straight line, the use of these two simple tones is as universal as Art itself. They appear in the black vine on the white marble floor of the Church of the Miracoli at Venice; on the wall of the Arabian Mosque, and the frieze of the Chinese temple. They have come into favor on book covers and page borders. Aubrey Beardsley went scarcely beyond them. R. Anning Bell and other artists have boldly carried them into pictorial work in the illustration of children's books.

These facts will demonstrate to the beginner that no terms are too simple for artistic genius to use. Moreover a limited field often stimulates to greater inventive activity.

EXERCISE

The principle of Variation comes into this exercise with special force, for each line-design admits of several Notan arrangements. The student should be given at first a pattern with few lines. Let him draw it from the instructor's sketch, or get it in any way that seems best, but the essential point is to have his design as good as possible in space-proportion be-

41

DARK-AND-
LIGH COM-
POSITION
X.—NOTAN
OF TWO
TONES—
STRAIGHT-
LINE PAT-
TERNS

fore he begins to add the ink wash. Having once obtained a good pencil drawing, let him make several tracings from it, and then darken certain spaces with clear black ink. A round Japanese brush, short and thick, will be needed for this work.

The examples show how this kind of problem has been handled.

RUGS

The Oriental rug suggests an excellent line-scheme for practice in Notan. Fortunately the Mohammedans have escaped the delusions of Realism, being forbidden by their religion to represent in their art any natural form. Their genius must express itself in abstract line — the geometric pattern — but they have Notan and color to help them.

Let the student design a rug with border and centre, the shapes to be pure inventions, with no reference whatever to nature. The border must be made to differ from the centre; this can be accomplished in many ways, even with black and white.

For instance:

Border: Black figures on white ground.
Centre: White figures on black ground.
Border: White figures on black ground.
Centre: Black figures on white ground.
Border: Small figures.
Centre: One large figure.
Border: Large figures.
Centre: Small surface pattern, etc.

Copying the design of some good rug would be valuable practice preliminary to this exercise.

The instructor will find it necessary to warn the students that mere inventive action is not art. Any one can, with patience, evolve a multitude of straight-line shapes that may serve in a rug border. No end of grotesque and ugly designs can be produced. The teacher must guide the young mind to perceive the difference between creating beautiful patterns, and mere fantastic play.

In like manner those little gifted with æsthetic perception may go far astray in following the two-tone idea. It is very easy and somewhat fascinating to darken parts of designs with black ink. The late poster craze showed to what depth of vulgarity this can be carried. The pupil must be taught that all two-tone arrangements are not fine, and that the very purpose of this exercise is to so develop his appreciation that he may be able to tell the difference between the good, the commonplace, and the ugly. His only guide must be his own innate taste, and his instructor's experience.

Nº 48 (ser 3er VI)

DARK-AND-LIGHT COMPOSITION

XI.—TWO TONES—VARIATION

BEAUTY of Line must underlie every Notan composition, and it should be said in this connection that beauty of Notan must underlie every color composition. The three elements have the closest relation to one another. For purposes of study, however, it is necessary to isolate each element, and even the separate principles of each.

In the present instance, Notan can be separated from Line, that is, the student's attention can be concentrated on Dark-and-Light only, by taking one line-design of acknowledged excellence and making many Notan variations of it; being sure of Beauty of Line, the only problem is to create Beauty of Notan.

Here, again, the so-called "historic ornament" can be used for its own inherent beauty, not for the study of a "style." These works of art are available to the beginner in five ways: the objects themselves, photographs, photographic reproductions, casts, and tracings. The lithographic illustrations and rude wood cuts in some books of design, being produced by mechanical, painstaking minds, are useless for our purpose here. They give no hint of the quality of the original. If the actual painting on an Egyptian mummy case is compared with a page of one of these books, the poor quality of the latter is instantly apparent. Chinese and Japanese "ornament" in most of such books is of the most flamboyant and decadent order.

The facsimile copies of Greek vases usually belong in this same category. On the other hand, these works of the mechanical copyist are of some use to persons familiar with the originals, or to those who can translate these hints of schemes into designs of their own.

The illustrations to this section are Notan variations on a Chinese fret, chosen for its excellent straight-line composition, and good proportion.

With these are shown similar variations of old textiles. Though we are not taking up Curved Line, it has been thought best to introduce these here as suggestions of ways of studying these beautiful relics of the art of past ages.

The student sketches or traces the outline of the textile pattern, and tries to discover how many fine two-tone arrangements can be made with it.

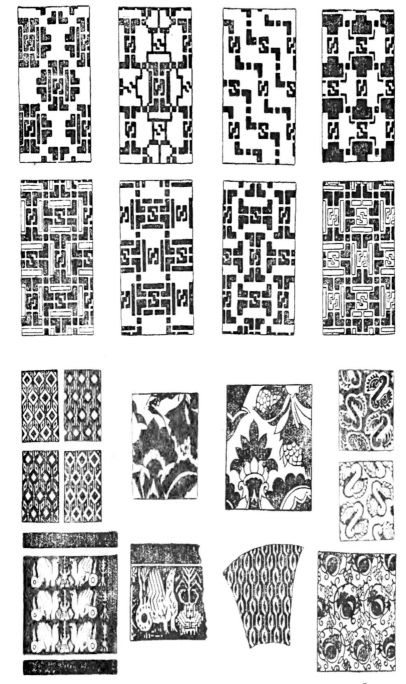

FLOWER COMPOSITION

XII.—LINE, AND NOTAN OF TWO TONES

FLOWERS, by their great variety of line and proportion, are particularly valuable, as well as convenient subjects for elementary composition. Their forms and colors have furnished themes for painters and sculptors since the beginning of Art, and the treatment has ranged from abstractions to extreme realism; from the refinements of lotus-derived friezes to the poppy and rose wall-papers of the present time.

In the exercise here suggested, there is no intention of making a design to apply to anything as decoration, hence there need be no question as to the amount of nature's truth to be introduced. The flower may be rendered realistically, as in some Japanese design, or reduced to an abstract suggestion, as in the Greek, without in the least affecting the purpose in view, namely, the setting of its lines into a space in such a way that beauty shall result—in other words, making it serve as a subject for a composition exercise.

It is essential that the space should be cut by the main lines. A small spray in the middle of a big oblong, or disconnected groups of flowers, cannot be called compositions; all the lines and areas must be related one to another by connections and placings, so as to form a beautiful whole. Not a picture of a flower is sought,—that can be left to the botanist—but rather an irregular pattern of lines and spaces, something far beyond the mere drawing of a flower from nature and laying an oblong over it, or vice versa.

EXERCISE

The instructor draws a flower in large firm outlines on the blackboard, avoiding confusing detail, and giving the character as simply as possible. The pupil first copies the instructor's drawing, then he decides upon the shape into which to compose this subject—a square or rectangle will be best for the beginner. He makes several trial arrangements roughly, with pencil or charcoal. Having chosen the best of these, he improves and refines them, first on his trial paper, and later by tracing with brush and ink on thin Japanese paper. Effort must be concentrated on the arrangement, not on botanical correctness.

Many line compositions can be derived from one flower subject, but each of these can in turn be made the source of a great variety of designs by carrying the exercise farther, into the field of Dark-and-Light. Paint certain of the areas black, and at once a whole new series suggests itself, from a single line design. To the beauty of the line is added the beauty of opposing and intermingling masses of black and white.

46

Japanese

Japanese

Japanese

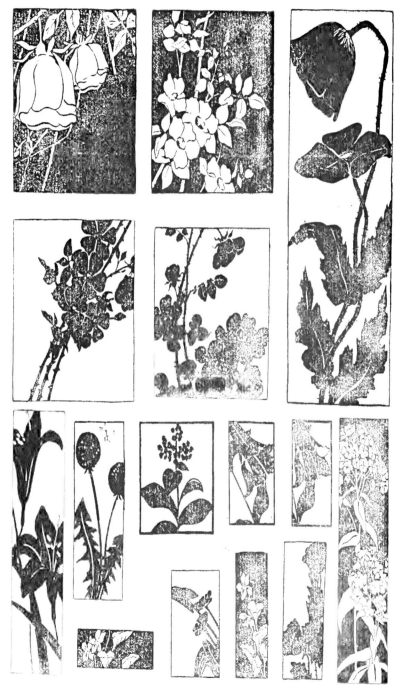

In this part of the exercise the arrangement of shapes of light with shapes of dark, occupies the attention, rather than shading, or the rendering of shadows. Hence the flowers and leaves and stems, or parts of them, may be black or white, according to the feeling of the student. Let him choose out of his several drawings those which he considers best. The instructor can then criticise, pointing out the best and the worst, and explaining why they are so. A mere aimless or mechanical blackening of paper, without effort to arrange, will result in nothing of value.

The examples show the variety of effects produced by flowers of different shapes, and the beauty resulting from schemes of Dark-and-Light in two tones. Pupils might profitably copy some of these, enlarging them; but only for preliminary practice. The instructor will, of course, use his own subject matter.

DARK-AND-LIGHT COMPOSITION

XIII.—NOTAN OF LANDSCAPE —TWO TONES

THE student has already experienced the composition of two tones with geometric line-design and flower-shapes; a step farther brings him to the important subject of Dark-and-Light as an element of Pictorial Art.

We must again emphasize the distinction between Light-and-Shadow, Light-and-Shade, and that which we here call Notan. Light-and-Shadow, a phenomenon connected with sunshine, can be expressed in pictorial art by means of Notan. That is, a combination of lights and shadows in nature is available to the artist only when their shapes occur in, or suggest, a beautiful arrangement; when they form, as it were, a pattern, or, as some would say, when they are "decorative." (This word is only a misleading circumlocution for "beautiful.") The student who is under the guidance of the academic phrase, "Paint what you see, and as you see it," feels that he must represent faithfully every accidental shadow, "just as it is in nature," or else be false to art and false to himself. He discovers later that such accurate rendering is only permissible in studies and sketches; that no accidents enter into pictures, but every line, every light, and every dark are a part of a deliberate design.

Light-and-Shade is a term referring mainly to the modelling of things, or the imitation of solidity. The study of it, as usually pursued in the schools by the drawing of white casts or still-life, tends to concentrate the students' attention upon the Representation of facts rather than the production of beauty. It does not help them to comprehend the æsthetic quality of, for instance, a charcoal sketch by William Morris Hunt. Moreover, to spend so much effort upon modelling is of doubtful value, for Painting is essentially the art of two dimensions.

When a painter makes roundness and solidity the chief aim of his work, he goes outside of his art and enters the province of his brother, the sculptor. In the best painting, for example, Giotto's frescoes at Assisi, Piero della Francesca's at Arezzo, Masaccio's "Tribute Money," the compositions of Vivarini, Bellini and Titian, and even the Strozzi portrait by Raphael, the modelling is entirely subordinate to the greater elements of proportion and Dark-and-Light.

In a mural painting extreme roundness is a fatal defect; a striking illustration is afforded in the Pantheon at Paris, where Puvis de Chavannes and his contemporaries have put their compositions on the walls. Puvis thought of his painting there as primarily a mosaic of colored shapes, whose mission was first of all to make the wall beautiful. No one thinks

DARK-AND-
LIGHT COM-
POSITION
XIII.— NO-
TAN OF
LANDSCAPE
— TWO
TONES

at first of the subject that he has put there, but all are charmed with the harmonies of line, tone, and color, the poetry and illusion of his landscape. The other painters seem to have thought mainly of modelling; of making their figures stand out solidly; and the result is that the beholder does not perceive the wall, or any suggestion of composition, but is entirely occupied with the sculpturesque reality of the painting. Soon he is confused by it and turns away unsatisfied.

But we do not wish to be misunderstood as advocating the entire omission of shadows, or of modelling—certain subjects may require their use—but the flat relations are of first importance; in them must lie the art of the painting.

Allusion has been made to the art students' practice of copying the darks from pictures, or the "spotting," as they call it. This is really studying Notan in two tones. To more fully define its purpose we give a few examples. No. 49 is a set of sketches from well-known masters showing the arrangement of Dark-and-Light reduced to two tones. This will give a hint of these artists' conception of the element of Notan, and it becomes more evident where translated into two tones. In Section XIX will be found some Japanese examples of the same thing. So interested were the Japanese in this kind of composition that they sketched and published in books the "spotting" of their great masters. Some of these books, particularly early ones of the period Genroku, are exceedingly beautiful.

EXERCISE

Give the student as a theme a landscape in line only, with no border. It should be simple, but with a variety of large and small spaces. Let this be handled in two ways:

1. The student sets it into a border, and when its proportions are satisfactory he traces it on several sheets of paper and tries the effect of painting certain spaces black. Some subjects are capable of a great many two-tone arrangements, but not all will be fine. Not number is required, but beauty.

2. Compose the landscape into borders of different proportions, then vary each of these with two tones.

The illustrations sufficiently explain both these ways of working.

No. 50 illustrates nine arrangements of one subject.

After using the examples here given, the student may sketch a landscape from nature, and after its line-composition has been criticised, let him vary it in two tones.

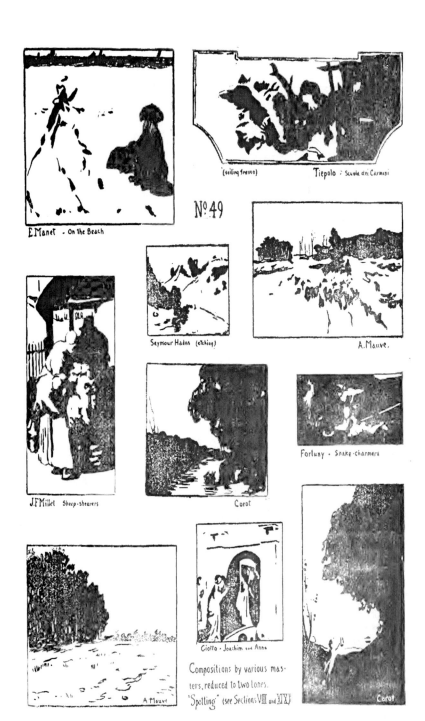

(ceiling fresco)

Tiepolo : Scuola dei Carmini

E. Manet - On the Beach

№ 49

Seymour Haden (etching)

A. Mauve.

J. F. Millet   Sheep-shearers

Corot

Fortuny - Snake-charmers

A. Mauve.

Giotto - Joachim and Anna

Compositions by various masters, reduced to two tones. "Spotting" (see Sections VIII and XIX)

Corot

No. 50
G. A. C.

BORDERS & SURFACE PATTERNS

XIV.—LINE AND NOTAN OF TWO TONES

IN Section VI Repetition was mentioned as one principle by which line-music may be composed; a simple kind of beauty to which even the savage gives expression, instinctively, by rows of lines upon his pottery or his blankets. (See No. 30, page 29). That primitive pattern easily developes into the design known as the "meander" or "Greek fret," one of the oldest ornamental devices. Its severe beauty is found in perfection in Greek design; but the Egyptians, Chinese, Aztecs, and others, the world over, have evolved innumerable variations of this straight-line theme.

EXERCISE

The problem before the student is the production of a rhythmical beauty in terms of straight line, to which shall afterward be added the beauty of Dark-and-Light.

The exercise may be carried out in two ways:

1. Taking as elements a row of straight marks, or lines and dots, | · | · | · | · | · develope, by means of repetition, both borders and surface patterns. No. 51 illustrates the manner of working. In this part of the exercise no area is enclosed by the lines; the beauty is that of a rhythmical marking off of space. This kind of design is particularly adapted to textile fabrics.

2. From the same row of marks, | | | | | | | | develope the meander as a border or a surface pattern. (No. 52.) Taking a suggestion from the Arabic designers, combine the lines in triangular, or irregular, arrangements. (No. 53.)

The Chinese fret in Section XI is an example of the second kind of composition. Beware of mere invention, without appreciation. To multiply marks on paper is just as easy as to drum on the piano. Repetition in itself does not constitute beauty; witness the bad wall-papers and other debased design—repetition of the meanest kind.

Invention is desirable, but a great number of designs thoughtlessly produced will be of no value. First make sure that the unit or the theme which you intend to repeat is itself beautiful. If it is composed of a few lines, see that they are well proportioned, one to the other, and delicately spaced. Then you may use Repetition to give a subtle quality of musical movement.

The line patterns may be translated into two tones. (See No. 54, etc.)

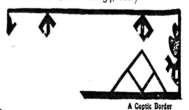

A Coptic Border

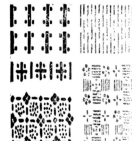

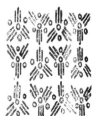

Nº51

Nº52

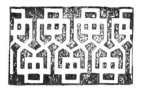

Nº54

Arabic border
(see page 31)

Nº53

FLOWER COMPOSITION

XV.—BORDERS IN TWO TONES

FLOWER composition was considered in Section XII purely as an exercise in the arrangement of shapes, with no reference to Applied Design. In this section, while arrangement is still the main point, the student can have in mind some practical use of the designs, either as borders, or head- and tail-pieces for books. But it is not necessary to take into account here all the limitations which such application might involve, as, for instance, the special handling for photographic reproduction, the disposition of masses required in perforated woodwork (to make it hold together) or the peculiar treatment of a stencil pattern. All these things can be considered by the student after he has had experience in art. If he has the art, its application will not be difficult; it is enough for him now to let the practical problem suggest a style of composition. In this case he may choose a long parallelogram, and work in both Line and Notan.

EXERCISE

The examples accompanying this exercise illustrate the idea suggested. These compositions can be worked out in charcoal or ink. Many small rough sketches or plans of the arrangement should be made first and the best of these chosen for further elaboration.

If desirable the single composition may be considered as a unit in a repeating border-pattern. The instructor should show the class how this kind of design has been used in magazines and other publications as a page-ornament.

FLOWER COMPOSITION

XVI.—TWO TONES—JAPANESE EXAMPLES

DEMONSTRATION by means of illustration is always a powerful means of impressing an idea upon the mind. In teaching young pupils the simple elements of composition, good examples are most essential.

Would that time had preserved for us the sketch-books of Phidias, of Giotto, of the architect of St. Mark's, of the great designers of textiles, buildings, and pictures. These are, for the most part, lost; the few scraps remaining are stored in museums. But the art of the East comes to our assistance with its sketch-books, its colored prints, and its paintings. The Japanese know of no such divisions as Representative and Decorative; they conceive of painting as the art of two dimensions; an art in which roundness and nature-imitation are subordinate to the flat relations. As in pre-Renaissance times in Europe, the education of the Japanese artist is founded upon composition. A thorough grounding in fundamental principles gives him the utmost freedom in designing. He loves nature and goes to her for

his subjects, but he does not imitate. The winding brook with wild iris (p. 37), the roadside weeds, the pebbles on the river-shore, are to him themes for his art, but he translates them into arrangements of Line, or Dark-and-Light, or Color. They are so many motifs for the division of a space into beautiful proportions, for harmonious line-systems, or sparkling inter-weavings of black and white. We are speaking now of the real art of Japan. The modern cheap imitation, the degraded commercial "art," made for the foreign market must be avoided.

The examples here given are reproduced from Japanese works of the best period, and from sheets of ancient designs. Their refinement of proportion, beauty of line-combination, strong drawing, and brilliancy of Notan need no comment.

Let the student enlarge them and vary their proportions. These will suggest to him one way of looking at nature, and of translating her beauty into the language of art.

BOOK COVERS, TITLE PAGES AND LETTERS

XVII.—LINE AND NOTAN OF TWO TONES

BOOK cover is a problem in rectangular arrangement. Whatever be the design placed upon it, the first question is the division into beautiful proportions. See Sections I, II, III, etc. Lettering may be considered as a tracery of Line or a pattern of Dark-and-Light; in fact it is itself a design, and the dignified beauty of simple lettering is often a sufficient ornament for a book cover. In any case the letters occupy a certain space, which must be well-proportioned. Above all, they must be clear and intelligible. Extravagance in lettering should be avoided, but variation is possible. Each letter may be reduced to its elements (as A to a set of three lines), and these varied like any line design. The title page, for our purpose here, is essentially the same problem as the cover.

INITIALS are a part of the Notan-scheme of a book-page. Considering the text as a gray tone, combined with a white margin, the initial comes between the two as a sort of focal point or accent, like the sharp touches of black in ancient Japanese ink-painting (see pages 11 and 39.) The initial itself is usually a composition in a somewhat square-shaped space—a useful subject for students if the scale be large.

EXERCISE

TUDENTS should make many small preliminary sketches for book covers, not attempting a large drawing till a definite and satisfactory plan of arrangement has been reached. Let them study good examples in the libraries. Reproductions or photographs of the fine old bindings will be valuable illustrations of dignity of style.

THE IMAGINARY MAGAZINE

A Collection of Designs
for Book Illustration
by Composition Class
of Pratt Institute.

No. I, December,
MDCCC XC VIII.

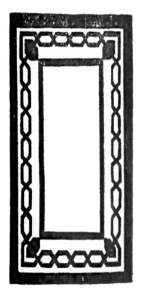

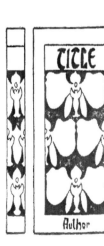

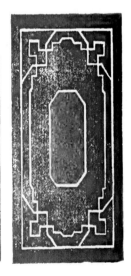

BOOK-PAGE COMPOSITION

XVIII.—TWO TONES—LANDSCAPE

THE art in book illustration lies not so much in "telling a story" as in beautifying the page. The page is a space into which the illustration is to be set; a problem of Line and Dark-and-Light, whose successful working out depends upon the illustrator's experience in composition. If the pictorial design is to have a rectangular boundary line, the setting of it upon the page is a matter of simple rectangular composition, as in Section II. If it is to be of irregular shape, its edges require special attention that their lines may be harmonious and may blend well with the type.

As a beginning in illustration the student ought first to practice setting an outline landscape upon a page, following this with the use of two tones (black and white). No. 55 exemplifies the outline work. No. 56, two tones with border. No. 57, two tones with no border.

N? 55

N? 57

T.H.L.

N? 56

C.L.M.

LANDSCAPE COMPOSITION

XIX.—TWO TONES—JAPANESE EXAMPLES

ALLUSION has already been made to the Japanese ink compositions (Section VIII), and Nos. 40, 41, and 42, are photographic reproductions of ink paintings by some of their masters. The two-tone landscape of Japanese art is found in books of sketches from old pictures, in books of sketchy studies, and in design books for stencilling cloth, for fretsaw work, etc. The sketches from old pictures date from the early days of painting, when only clear black was used (Nos. 58, 59, 60, 61). They are, in fact, studies in "spotting," to aid the memory of those who had seen the originals, or to suggest to others the general arrangement of the masses in the masterpieces. The quality of these old books with their age-stained paper and velvety gray-black ink cannot be reproduced, but these illustrations may stimulate the student to investigate for himself.

Nos. 62, 63, and the rest, are examples of more recent date, but of great interest for their naive composition, their beauty of Line and Notan.

The student should copy these, enlarge and vary them.

No 58

Two sketches of compositions by old masters

Japanese book of XVIII cent

Nº 59   From Japanese book, XVIII century

N°60

N°61 The "spotting" of a picture by Sesshu,
(from a sketch-book of the Tanyu school)
see pages 9,10,37,39, also p. 53.

N°62　N°63

Original compo
sitions from a
sketch-book of
the Shijo school

DARK-AND-LIGHT COMPOSITION

XX. — THREE TONES

CLEAR black against clear white is a strong contrast, and even the best work in these tones has a certain harshness, despite its sparkling brilliancy. But the introduction of a tone of gray, midway between these two extremes changes the conditions radically, and opens up a whole new class of creative possibilities. With these three tones comes the beauty of different degrees of Notan, the "value" of one tone against another. This simple set of three tones is the basis of the mezzotint, the charcoal sketch, the aquatint, and the wash-drawing. In this class belong the old masters' drawings on gray paper with black and white.

From three tones it is easy to develope compositions into many tones, and in these refinements of the great element of Notan lies the true meaning of the word "Values." This word in modern art-education is restricted to that property of painted objects whereby they take their places one beyond another in the picture. While this is a desirable quality in pictorial art, it is nevertheless a quality belonging to Representation, not to Beauty, and in its extreme manifestation becomes a species of deception most agreeable to the mind unappreciative of art. The multitude who have no perception of harmonies of tone and color are delighted to see objects "stand out" in the picture "as if they were real." But the word "values" in its broadest and truest sense refers to beauty only; the value of a tone is its lightness or darkness by which it affects the tone next to it.

In three-tone work a new exercise of judgment is involved, that of determining the value of the medium tone. The student has to mix this tone and decide when it is of the right depth. Here he begins really to paint for the first time.

EXERCISE

For this painting-exercise will be needed two new kinds of materials — a white plate, or set of dishes (corresponding to the palette in oil painting) on which to mix the ink tones — and flat Japanese brushes. The first difficulty to overcome is the laying of a flat wash, a problem of water-color painting requiring dexterity and much practice. For a space of considerable size a flat brush is preferable to a round one. As to paper the best results are produced on a well-sized Japanese paper of fine quality. The thin coating of glue keeps the edge of the wash from drying in before the brush can take it up.

For a beginning choose a simple straight-line pattern, decide which parts of it shall be white, and wash a medium tone of gray over the rest. When dry, paint in the black spaces. A clean ink-stone, clean plate, and clean brush are essential to success.

68

To illustrate Sec XXI
page 72

The reason for keeping the tones flat is that the value of a whole space can best be judged when it is flat. If it is sloppy and uneven it loses force and interest. In beginners' work and in decorative design flatness is necessary. But of course in ac- tual picture-painting the absolutely flat tone would rarely be used.

(Note. Many of the three-tone illustra- tions were drawn upon "scratch-board" for convenience of reproduction — in this case the fine lines stand for the gray wash.)

Composition by Ribot - see Section VIII
also pages 39 and 40

DARK-AND-LIGHT COMPOSITION

XXI.—THREE TONES—FLOWERS

THE examples with this section sufficiently explain themselves. A comparison of these with the flowers in two tones will at once make evident the new kind of delicate beauty that the third tone introduces.

Designs such as these could easily find a place in book-illustration.

The irregular shapes in flower composition will probably necessitate the use of the round, pointed brush in putting on the washes.

The pen-lines represent the flat ink-wash

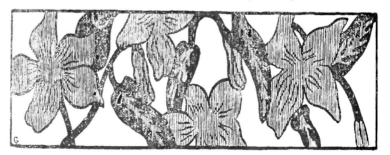

Flowers to il-
lustrate Sec XXI
see p p. 70. 72.

Landscapes to il-
lustrate Sec XXII
see p p. 71.75

DARK-AND-LIGHT COMPOSITION

XXII. — THREE TONES — LANDSCAPE

IN applying three tones to pictorial art we go a step beyond the two previous exercises, for this brings us almost to the expression of effects of nature like gray days and twilight.

Still the student should, for the present, consider his landscape as a pattern or mosaic of varying tones, regardless of questions of realistic truth. As in all his work, beauty of arrangement must engage his attention above all else.

Many illustrators have produced the third tone in black and white work by means of closely-spaced pen lines. This has the advantage of being easily reproduced.

EXERCISE

For three-tone landscape the pupil can use Japanese ink and wash as in the last exercise, or pen and ink with fine lines for the third tone, or charcoal. In the latter case put a tone over the whole paper, take out the lights with bread or rubber, and draw in the darks with very black charcoal. This is closely allied to the process of mezzotint and aquatint.

It is perhaps unnecessary to suggest that a wide scope can be given this exercise by varying each landscape attempted, and that the student should draw one of his own from nature and treat it in the same way.

BOOK ILLUSTRATION

XXIII. — THREE TONES — AN IMAGINARY **POEM**

THIS will be a practical application of the foregoing lessons in composition. It comprises the arrangement of verses of poetry, a title in large type, and a landscape, upon a magazine page. It seems a complicated affair, but is really little more than a simple arrangement of areas, like Sections I and II. The text may be represented by a flat gray wash. The edges of the page are the boundaries of the composition, a parallelogram. If the verses, the lettering and the pictorial part are enclosed in rectangles, then the case is similar to some of our first exercises, and may be made a severe, symmetrical arrangement. But whether the different parts are regular or irregular, the problem is to set them together harmoniously. The best illustrative work is characterized by restraint, dignity and simplicity. The whole page must be one complete composition. Students must avoid strange, pseudo-Japanese combinations, such as scroll-like shapes, imitations of turned-down corners, or meaningless sprays of flowers. Keep to plain simple masses, beautiful in proportion and tone.

MORNING IN THE MARSHES

THE OLD MILL

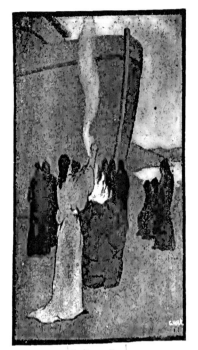

Noah's sacrifice

ADVANCED COMPOSITION

XXIV. — MANY TONES

LINE, Notan, and Color may be called the language of the art of Painting. Like the language of speech it may be used well or ill, to voice noble emotions in the beauty of poetic style, or to subserve the vulgar and the commonplace. There can be no æsthetic quality in this language unless it conforms to the requirements of art. A number of facts, accurately described in paint and color, may have no more connection with art than a similar set of written statements — merely plain prose. There is no art in such things unless the statements are bound together by certain subtle relations which we call beauty. When beauty enters, the parts cease to have a separate existence, but are melted together into a unit.

Advanced composition is only a working out of simple elements into more complex and difficult interrelations. If the picture has figures and landscape, the lines of the figures and the lines of the landscape run in such directions, intersect and interweave in such ways as to form a musical movement. The tones and the colors are so arranged as to mutually enrich one another. A noble subject for a picture requires nobility of style in its expression. Michelangelo's line (No. 11) is as grand as his subject. We do not presume to define Beauty or to attempt its description in words. Its nature must be learned by experience and by the study of the best works.

Beauty of Line is illustrated at the beginning of this book (pages 7, 9, 10, 11, 12 and 13); many other painters are distinguished for this quality, for example, Ririomin (Chinese, 11th century), Vivarini, and the designers of the best stained glass, Dürer, Holbein, and the great etchers.

Beauty of Notan is found in perfection as has been said before, in the works of the old Chinese and Japanese masters (pages 39,40,65,66,67). Rembrandt, Turner, William Morris Hunt, and again the etchers, can also be studied for this kind of language. (See Sec. VIII.)

Beauty of color has its highest development in the Venetian school; one hesitates to specify, but two noble examples might be mentioned, the "Santa Barbara" of Palma Vecchio, and "The Rich Man and Lazarus" of Bonifacio Veronese. In the modern French school, if one were to be singled out whose color is pre-eminent, it would be Albert Besnard.

In Japanese art the greatest masters of this language are Nobuzane (13th century), Korin (early 18th), and particularly the color-print artists, from Hishikawa Moronobu to Hiroshige.

ADVANCED
COMPOSI-
TION
XXIV.—
MANY
TONES

This section is illustrated with a few sketches for pictures, worked out in charcoal by young students in the author's classes at Pratt Institute. Their training in this new system of art education has enabled them to conceive of a subject in a few planes and simple masses — to keep in mind the underlying ideas of composition — to think of a picture first as pure design, secondly and subordinately as Representation.

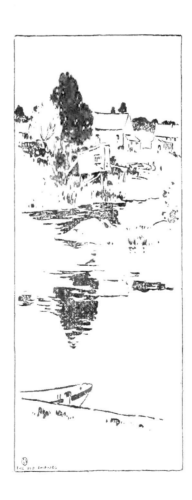

Druid priests worshipping at sunrise

The Departure of the old Year

Druid priests worshipping at sunrise

The Rainy Day

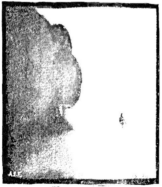

Through the portals of the sunset

Sketch in three tones

CONCLUSION OF THE FIRST PART

I HAVE called this book Part I, because other treatises may follow, taking up the subjects more in detail, including principles not here mentioned, and giving still fuller illustration of the system's development in Line, Notan and Color.

I have purposely kept to a broad and general survey of the field of composition, as a more detailed consideration of principles at this time, with their names, might lead to misunderstanding. The words Opposition, Transition, Subordination, Balance, Dark-and-Light, etc., though common words, were first used by the author of this system to designate certain special kinds of beauty, or ways of composing; hence, in order to be rightly understood and used, they need special explanation and illustration, for which there is no space in this small volume. For instance, Opposition is a great constructive idea, expressing severity, calm, solemnity, grandeur; it is embodied in the Egyptian temple, the Parthenon, the majestic paintings of Puvis de Chavannes. To think of it as a mere geometric right angle is entirely to misunderstand its meaning. To really comprehend such a principle means full knowledge of its use in the art of the world, and actual experience with it as a mode of expression. Such a detailed study of this and other principles will be undertaken in some succeeding volume. The aim of this Part I has been to suggest a line of practical work, which would make clearer the so-called vague subject of Composition.

Japanese (see page 61)

ImTheStory.com

Personalized Classic Books in many genre's

Unique gift for kids, partners, friends, colleagues

Customize:

- Character Names
- Upload your own front/back cover images (optional)
- Inscribe a personal message/dedication on the
  inside page (optional)

Customize many titles Including

- Alice in Wonderland
- Romeo and Juliet
- The Wizard of Oz
- A Christmas Carol
- Dracula
- Dr. Jekyll & Mr. Hyde
- And more...

CPSIA information can be obtained at www.ICGtesting.com
Printed in the USA
BVOW05s0856020516

446398BV00017B/112/P